COURSE

COURSE

Athena Kildegaard

TINDERBOX
EDITIONS

Tinderbox Editions
Molly Sutton Kiefer, Publisher and Editor
Red Wing, Minnesota
tinderboxeditions@gmail.com
www.tinderboxeditions.org

Cover design by Nikkita Cohoon
Cover art by Chris Maynard, "Give and Take," argus pheasant tail support
    feathers, 24" x 19," 2016.
Interior design by Nikkita Cohoon
Author photo by Arne Kildegaard

Athena Kildegaard is a fiscal year 2018 recipient of an Artist Initiative grant from the Minnesota State Arts Board. This activity is made possible by the voters of Minnesota through a grant from the Minnesota State Arts Board, thanks to a legislative appropriation from the arts and cultural heritage fund.

MINNESOTA
STATE ARTS BOARD

CLEAN
WATER
LAND &
LEGACY
AMENDMENT

In Memoriam
Kathleen Celeste Huber Owen
(1933 - 2009)

For Papa

Something is taking its course.

—Samuel Beckett

In its beginning, it is not yet the River;
in its end, it is no longer the River.

—T.S. Eliot

Contents

3 : SHARP DISTANCE

4 : DETOUR

5 : FROM THE SHADOW

6 : WEIGHT OF A BODY

COURSE

1: What signal

COURSES ON THE RIVER

*

Teach me
to plumb your current,
teach me to surface.

*

Current casts
no shadow,
is its own detour.

*

Turtle surfaces, tries the bank,
returns to water—
here or there just the same.

DEPARTURE

I smelled it first, a rot
flies delight in, a wavering
and deep-muddy smell,
for the turtle was pretty well
reduced, its eyes keyholes,
its spiny tail loosed from ruddering.

Left by a fisherman, the turtle
was big on the rocks
above the river. It must have
flailed, nothing to hold on to,
balanced as it was on granite,
soundless and paddling—
with its talony feet—the air.

The flies revived the body. I left them all
on that flinty shore.

I HAD TO WAIT

The way the deer regarded me—
pensive as an urn,
other-worldly,
risen—

turned me inside out—

and after she'd bounded—
her white tail
pulsing
among the birches—

I had to wait—
shivering,
as if I'd come up
out of water—

SNAKE

On the path
it slips
below matte
of last year's growth.

Downwind
it laps
upon itself
whorled on granite
lapping sun.

Decades ago
my mother told me
Navajo could walk
without sound. Like
beetles or meteors.

I practice. The snake pours
its tight body
over the edge.

ASTERS

All July and August they stand
for themselves, tilt in wind,
and fade, quiet as long-gone stars.

Seen close, a star ravishes.
Half a billion years from now
it implodes, self-ravishment.

White asters, thin-petaled
and drought-abiding, die in autumn,
sleep late, rise slowly.

WHAT TEMPERS US

On the gazebo floor, below a nest
packed tight against a rafter,
a nestling swallow, pink
and slippery blue,
lay stiff in death.

Two nights before, a storm
brought the river past its banks
and a cottonwood down
heavy against milkweed.

I was mesmered by the swallow parent
circling closer and chiding, until she
lit on the railing opposite,
turned her left eye on me.

Her orange breast fretted,
she lifted one slender claw
and then the other,
afraid to stay, afraid to go.
I should have gone.

But I wanted to see the last chicks leap.
Their thin beaks were lined flag-white;
they watched me with one eye
and didn't move.

THREE SCENES IN SEARCH
OF HISTORY

i.

Seven snow geese—their voices the muffled
mumbling of sleepers—fly overhead,
bank west, then north, and in that maneuver
flash white, a tender flaunting, a flush.

ii.

I have never stepped into a rose garden without
hungering for the past. Nor have I worn
my mother's purple shawl, her cotton night gown,
her turquoise, without feeling some truth.

iii.

Two deer arrive from reeds to the west,
meander on the snowy path. On through bluestem
and blown milkweed they go, toward
the bur oak grove where last year barred owls nested.

iv.

Nasturtium flowers face the sun unabashed.
Their leaves are yellow. Your letter hasn't arrived. Or
you haven't written. I know about waiting, how footsteps
in that emptiness twang, how there's no history.

v.

The snow geese right and are gone.
I go on leaving the house. I am grateful
for old roses, how they stay past first frost. How
they smell of propriety, of the chances we take.

vi.

A raccoon leaves its sharp-toed prints
on the deers' cloven moons. A pheasant crosses.
Woman, rodent, ungulate, snow, earth, all
the way down. The echoes are small insights.

ASYLUM

Herons built a rookery
in cottonwoods,
a slough on either side.

Half a century ago
men from the state hospital—
the gentle inmates—
came down from the river and built shacks
of corrugated and rusting sheets,
warped boards allocated by the superintendent,
washed up styrofoam, cracked shingles, mud.
Trees and curtains of vines
made solitude.
No electricity, no running water,
nothing but days on days in murky light,
the tang of wild grapes,
of private pleasures.

The herons—several dozen pairs—
put their slapdash nests
in only a few trees
so close together the young
eyeballed one another
to see who would fly first.

The quiet men sometimes
wandered singly into town
along the shoulder,
their bodies covered in gray and brown,
the draft of trucks
lifting their hems and cuffs.

They returned with matches
and kerosene and jars of jam
and girlie calendars.

Then the rules changed.
The last man from the river,
forced back to the ward,
died soon after, an exile.

The heron fledglings dropped
from the nests and flew. That
was that. The last adult
lifted her yellow legs, her yellow feet,
the branch swayed a little,
swayed lithe and green
and then returned
to its state of rest.

ELEMENTAL (I)

All across the landscape, after spring rains,
prairie potholes appear like stars.
Winter wore us down to need.
Coots and geese, mergansers, swim
between fallow fields—and two swans

dip past reeds, through clouds
to tender muck-thriving stems and leaves.
Ripples the birds make lend the water gravitas,
as constellations do the sky. The birds bob up,
dive again, take flight. Thus we doubt

our own galactic path. A farmer steers
his churring green machine down plumb rows.
We lollygag on the shoulder, windows down,
wait for the dark, as astronomers do.
We orbit awhile, drive off, mile becoming mile.

WHAT CAN BE MADE OF NOTHING

Blackbirds bunch
the water-sopped
pothole,

stand
on cattails,
pleasure the air,
whistle,

lift wing
all afternoon,
press beak
along quill

lackadaisical.
What signal,
what shot
will start them?

They loiter,
the thousand
reed-hidden
blackbirds.

NOTHING STAYS THE SAME ON THE RIVER

Great blue herons
surge high
past the sloughs

and are gone.
Swallows fall
from the bridge's eaves.

They skim for bugs
then return
to their earthy nests—

crimped clay wombs
or eye sacs—
pockets into which

the swallows
reach wormy beaks.
The river has muscled

the banks right up
to where salyx
shiver down pollen.

SPEAK TO THE EARTH

It is possible to capture a swarm
of wild bees—
nail a box high on a tree,
swab it with lemongrass oil—

and practice the patience of Job.

Until the bet, Job had no need
of patience. All good things
came to him with the ease of wind.

Happy is the man whom God correcteth.

A million bees died at once,
more than a million
at one commercial keeper's.

Cannot my tongue taste perverse things?
Job asked his friends, wagging a bit,
loosening up for later.

And what counts as perverse?

The drones go out ahead
of the new queen. If your box
is in their path, good news.

What is man, that thou shouldest
magnify him? And that thou shouldest
set thine heart upon him?
Job asked his God. He was covered in boils,
lost among men, patient in his love.

But, too: I am full of confusion.

If the drones do not find your box
you must try again next year.

Job said to God: Thou hast fenced me
with bones and sinews.

Our bodies hold us in.

Why do the bees hurry away
all together, congregants in the earth,
their own sinews
delineating their sashes of gold?

And Job said: I went mourning without the sun.

But should the drones find your box baited
with lemon grass oil, be ready. You have been waiting.
Lift the box down, move it span
by span to where you can
steward the hive.

Speak to the earth,
and it shall teach thee,
Job said to his friends.

TENDERNESS

I am driving toward the house of a friend
to move furniture,
to make a place for death.

Last night a fawn vaulted the hood
(inside: me, my husband, my son, his girl)
and fell to the ditch. I cried to the dead.

Today a fawn by the road looks
at me—I've barely started,
barely prepared for the dying—

its white spots clouds
or stars. I plead once, not to my friend or her man,
but to the dead. (Mother.)

This state highway, that gravel road,
this carved bed, that rocking chair (boundless),
any tender place a place for death.

2: Get a body through

COURSES ON THE RIVER

Such restlessness—
the river moves
and doesn't move.

*

I know the heron
by shadow
coursing over sandbar.

*

The river folds itself
around any body—
cloud, ash, heron's shadow.

IN A PHOTO ALBUM

Late August sun flares hot
on the window pane. Weeds beside
the white house throw their shadows,
duplicate themselves, feign abundance.
Sun flares in the one window.

It is on fire. My mother stands below
in curls and tied white shoes,
an only child, plump and solid.
She offers her birthday doll
to the emptiness between us.

The shadow—girl and doll—grows
strange against the white house,
beside the flourishing weeds,
below the one window where sun gongs
and gongs against the pane.

MORNINGS BEFORE THE TEXAS HIGH-NOON HEAT

My mother hauled the white plastic basket to the yard,
an apron with pockets full of wooden pins
tied around her post-partum waist. She set the basket
down in yellow mortal grass, the smell of bleach
stirring up from hard-wrung cloth. But first
she had to move along the lines plucking
slugs from their precarious perches, shiny
acrobats stretched out in slender viscous arcs
high and clean in the dry morning air.
Each one she plucked, dozens of them some days,
she threw down, smashed with her shoe,
one silken body at a time, pressing each
into the red dirt. And when she'd cleared
the slugs she stroked a cloth along the lines
before shaking out panties, handkerchiefs,
white shirts, pillowcases, her Sunday dress,
washcloths and teatowels, diapers, draping their corners
lightly, pinning them fast, and then going
back into the house to wash her hands, to start
another load, sit before a fan, her skirt
pulled up above her knees, and cool down
enough to move to the piano where she
practiced Chopin while the washer spun and
the sun cast human shadows across the silver smudges.

SONG

At any given time she only owned
one sturdy bra. After awhile white rubber threads
escaped the cotton shell, and the shoulder straps

curled in delicate scallops over her shoulder.
She bowed to settle her breasts into the cups.
Her father, a preacher who believed

in the virtue of thrift, allowed one square
of toilet tissue, three, if necessary. His pencils,
she told us many times—as if, though he died

when she was young, she still could not believe—
he arranged by size, each sharp as the poison of certainty.
From the alley on winter school-day afternoons

in the cold and hoary dark I watched her
in the haloed light of the stove's hood.
I could see her contentment

or her anger in how she bent to her task. She'd
woven a nest of silence and dark around herself.
I wanted to enter it a pilgrim but did not know how.

CURSING THE COLD

She moved from the heat of the Canadian breaks,
from proper Baptist country where women wore hose
and girdles when they left the house, to St. Peter,
where mules once dragged barges against the current
and houses had secret basement doors to tunnels
to escape the Sioux, or so it was said. She took
us scavenging for elderberries, muscadine, gooseberries,
and one lucky spring we found morels. But
she grew cold, couldn't shake the cold, or the way
women met to drink and smoke without wearing
brassieres or shoes with heels. How many times
did she tell the story of arriving at her first ladies'
luncheon in a black worsted suit and pearls? How many
times did she curse winter, curse the overcast below-zero
days of February, curse the catered dinners of chicken Kiev
rubber-stiff and bleeding pale fat, curse the stolid
Swedes who called black-eyed peas cow peas because
they knew nothing of collards and cream gravy
and cornbread made with buttermilk, the food that could
get a body through drought and dust storm and revival meetings
and almost, if you sang Abide with Me or Grace, Grace,
God's Grace, friends and family around you sharing hymnals,
the young women trying the descant, your husband
wanting to stop a verse too soon, before the resurrection,
before the unnamed shame, you weeping even though
you didn't believe, because the ghosts arrived, they had come
north too, if you crossed over into the music, there might be
enough to get your body through the long cold.

NOCTURNE FOR JANUARY, 1965

The blue Rambler with a back seat narrow
as a hospital bed, and a snow plow

met on Hwy 169, halfway to town.
A blizzard hampered the world.

They'd gone for butter, pork chops, a liter
of bourbon, when the plow slipped

across the lane. Insurance didn't cover it.
The gash rusted. Until April, snow sifted

onto the wool upholstery. How brash
my parents were then. *No time*

to wonder why, Whoopee! We're all gonna die.
How beautiful they were, how boundless.

ELEMENTAL (2)

She pulled water
from a bowl, flicked it
across a shirt, a napkin, an apron—

and rolled each
into damp fists.

I ironed handkerchiefs—
my fathers', white cotton
without embellishment,
the sort that came in packages of ten
from the five and dime.
Iron, fold, iron, fold
down to perfect squares—
geometry to heal loneliness.

When I no longer needed
a box to stand on
I ironed my father's dress shirts,
my mother's blouses—
collars and darts small challenges—
skirts with box pleats,
and the black and white
cutwork tablecloth she labored at
two winters, the linen heaped
in her lap
like a cat or a warming stone.

No, I did not iron that cloth
for it came out of the linen closet
only that once.

EVENING RITE

I would walk from my bedroom, once a cook's,
past the kitchen stairs, around a corner
to enter my parents' bedroom where
I liked to watch my mother dress
for a night out.

         Once her girdle was in place
and her hose latched by satin straps, she'd
take up her mother's wood-handled brush
(a brush she once used to straighten up
my brother) and she'd bend over, the flesh
below her breasts rolling over the top of the girdle,
and she'd brush her hair in long strokes
from her nape across the back of her head
and forward right to the ends of the hair,
hair that spread black and shiny, and in winter
sparks would flash as she brushed, winter dark stars,
and if she was not in a hurry I could stand
beside her and take the brush and lead it
through her beautiful hair, the smell of earth
rising up like fog on water,
my free hand on the cool rise of her back.

TRIPS SOUTH

With the window cracked, his shoulder
tucked against the door, he drove, the radio tuned
to classical stations out of Omaha, Saint Louis,
Amarillo, if he could find one, or Hank Williams,
Johnny Cash, corn futures, baseball, and late
at night a Baptist preacher with a toll-free

number and a prayer. He drove with the back
of my mother's hand—the thick gold band heavy
and loose on her ring finger—touching his shoulder,
since she'd thrown her arm along the back
of the front seat. She could steady him and then
belt us with one quick flick if we bickered.

They'd play at guessing the composer,
the conductor, which philharmonic, joshing
one another, showing off a little what they knew,
though my mother was right most often.
They took turns smoking. Sometimes we'd all
sing Stephen Foster. My father drove the whole way.

SUMMER LABORS

My mother had stretched wool
from breast beam to iron heddles
and raised the windows

to a hickory whose leaves
curled in the summer heat.
Her back straight to relieve her hips,

she leaned into the loom.
In the other room—a room
with a white marble fireplace,

its curves of acanthus leaves
arctic in the Minnesota humidity—
I practiced Haydn, an allegro,

the metronome incorrigible.
Between throwing the shuttle and beating
the weft she called to me

about a missed flat or how I must
play the D with my third finger,
something I later realized she knew

because I stumbled two notes later.
And still I stumble. And still I sit taller
to relieve her stubborn desire, or perhaps my own.

FOR BODY CRAVING WARMTH

She dreamt of giving birth
to cats. The doctor placed the wet
kittens on her belly. Once, she called
to tell me how she'd watched

a sparrow hawk drop to break
a songbird's neck and eat it.
Her father built a cage to house
the wounded she would nurse

until a starling slashed itself
to death against a wire, the cage
no place for it. When bats
from the river came in, lost,

she closed herself in the pantry,
waited under the strong bulb,
in the hot light. In the heat
of her lap, her cat curled, at the end.

ON THE RIVER AFTER THE SUN GOES DOWN

When we children nestled against
one another and the moon's light made
the sand-bar we were on seem as if it would pull away
and float downriver with all of us aboard,
when the men unrolled their pant legs
and the women, our mother included, were thinking
of removing blouses, all of you poured
another glass of booze—no ice, long since melted—and lit
a cigarette, or lit one another's, a come on, a tease,
because she was not sitting next to our father, he was
across the fire, and she was tipsy, everyone was tipsy,
and warm still from the August sun, August before
the men went back to teaching co-eds and radicals, so
you all inhaled and exhaled and between smoking
you disagreed about will, whether we have a will,
because it seemed then that someone had reduced
our brains to instinct, the psychologist explained,
and it got exciting, the disagreement, the anxiety,
since that was what you were feeling, that maybe it's true,
this cigarette is not a choice, the man you'd never
really looked at before, the man next to you who
lit your cigarette, or you lit his, is handsome
in the bonfire's pulse, and you are sated,
absolutely sated with pleasure.

BATH

On the tub's edge she balanced
an ashtray and a sweating glass of bourbon.
On plum-colored rubber-backed rugs
my girlfriends and I sat, unsprung like grasshoppers
in the tight space. Our lungs filled
with nicotine and lavender bath salts
and the barreled tang of liquor. I never told
she was afraid of swimming. When the water
cooled she levered open the drain, grew pimply
while the water level dropped, snapped the drain shut,
refilled. Her breasts rose and fell as she moved,
skiffs of bubbles harbored around her knees.
She smoked steadily and we confessed our troubles.

NOCTURNE FOR 1975

Booze-sopped friends shouted down bullies in Washington
and stacked the hi-fi with Dylan, Cream,

Herb Alpert, music my mother couldn't stomach,
and the woman my father trifled with laughed

so loud it carried right through that upright
and high-ceilinged house, its walls thick enough to hide

a corpse. They went away and my father passed out.
She heaved gin and clotted cheese,

heaved dozens of pills, tiny white
and pink and beautiful into a bowl.

ELEMENTAL (3)

Sometimes, when I play—
an invention, say, or a nocturne—
I catch sight of her hands on the keys.

She pounded veal and threw
a shuttle, played Liszt and Chopin,
painted damask roses, darned socks,

read palms. Mine, finally, I'd begged enough.
My hand in hers: perhaps she agreed
for the heat. My right warming her left.

She stroked the lines and mounts,
folded out the map of my fingers.
When I was born she cried—her hand
couching mine—because I looked like her.

I GIVE VOICE TO MY MOTHER
AND SHE EXPLAINS SOMETHING

Seven years after Daddy died, when I was twenty,
I came that close, gas filling our apartment,
my mother in that funny Amarillo kitchen
near death too. I phoned out, windows were thrown open.

When I was small my mother let me sit
behind her, wrap my arms around to nest
my hands below her naked breasts. We sang
Swing Low and In the Sweet By and By,
her filling diaphragm pushing my hands,
my hands her breasts. We kept the rhythm jointly.

That gas took me with it. My stranger heart
knocked impertinent, eager, and entered. In that
brief death and in the next, my hands are couched
below my mother's incorruptible bosom.

A STORY SHE TOLD MANY TIMES

How near to death,
how simple
and acceptable.

(Count yourself lucky.)

How eager she seemed,
her body a cold cage—
no place for her,
the body corruptible, as in rust,
as in the slashing of nicotine,
a desperation.

Whose body is this body?

Do we not all long
to place our hands
below our mother's breasts?

How she sometimes
regretted that phone call.

How easy to be betrayed.

ELEMENTAL (4)

In another time you might have been
crammed into a bag and dropped
in a fjord or bog, or burned, or stoned.

You read palms and revealed bitter
truths or small shames or hope. This
was not a party game. This was necessary.

You quit a singing career to nurture
small children, yours, others', and rapists kept
safe at the state hospital and, finally,

families of drunks—wives, mostly, like you—
who'd come close to drowning, who'd seen
things not revealed to most of us.

In another time, cavorting with tots
and criminals, the ravening, and cats,
cavorting, even in dreams, with cats,

was blasphemy. What you knew was necessary
was to listen to the innocent,
the violent, the wounded, to give them refuge.

THE RIVER SPEAKS TO MY MOTHER

There's nowhere you can't go,
can't be, swirl or ripple,
drift of seed, pad of lichen,
round the sandbar's bend
come morning, come night,
slip into current easy as mink,
let catfish pull you in
and through as if you were
thread connecting hyssop
and anemone to bunged cypress,
connecting paddle boat to bridge
and floating dock, all the dogs
wet and sleeked to thrills,
dragonflies zipped and crazy,
cottonmouths dreaming whorls,
all the barred owls sleeping
one-eyed, waking open-fisted,
all the mornings shedding twist,
high noon slapping down
a winning hand, nights thick
with mosquitoes and violins,
there's nowhere you can't be,
limestone bluff, reed-thick slough,
moss-slipped slate, driftwood bank,
voodoo queen, catfish gut, muskrat
den, death-grip falls, muscadine
shade, oxbow and flood plain,
lock and dam, baptismal waters,
sluice and channel, churn and scar,
heron pool, iron-doused
cavern, tabernacle all the way

north to south, all the way hotter,
hot as Hades, all the way
hot enough to get your body through.

3: Sharp distance

COURSES ON THE RIVER

Swallows soar
across burnished water.
Waves fold the shadows' paths.

*

Days of no rain—
roots of a cottonwood above water.

Rain overnight—the tree's submerged—
have I changed so soon?

*

Along the bank—sunlight
makes flowers of leaves.
How vain to seek certainty.

THE SHARP DISTANCE (1)

You'd gone back
to Texas for the winter.
A plumb-line down the continent.

You ate a half dish of squid—
from the depths a swimming creature
of such silken and sleek beauty,

soul-replete, it moved
with the currents of your body.
The night before

we talked by phone.
I didn't dream of you.
The squid grew still in your embrace.

CADENCE

Pain just there, same
place as a month ago.
You wouldn't obey
the doctors, you said
on the phone, you'd go
home to Scarlatti
and Brahms, to Minnie
purring in your lap,
you'd insist on the long
strains between breaths,
the pizzicati of oxygen.

At the end—my father told
me on the phone—you gave
yourself to your body,
every breath a mark
on time's surface, a shallow
etching, shallower each one,
as if a needle were rising
from the groove,
the cat purring on your lap,
your hand in my father's,
even at the end the cat
purring in your warmth,
and your eyes lifted upward
to see what was taking
its course, to see beyond
your body, as if
to witness your own cadence.

THE SHARP DISTANCE (2)

Out the window I saw
my own footsteps
cross thin snow.
Three days earlier

I fed birds who don't
mind cold: juncoes, chickadees.
I stopped half-way. My shoes
pressed through to green,

my lungs sated with
sharp air. I sought
enough cold to mind
the sharp distance.

LOOKING FOR THE PARTICULAR, AN INVENTION

1.

My sister and I stood surrounded
by pastel jars and low tubs of whipped cloud
and tubes of tinselled gels. We tried every tester
up and down our arms, on our hands, lilac,
myrrh, frangipani, lemongrass, gardenia.
We leaned into the spritz of bubbles. We laughed,
made fools of ourselves, until a shop girl,
earnest as an obituary, asked
were we looking for anything particular.

How many times have we done this, my sister,
our mother, and me? But not this time.
This I've invented. Because I was not there
to wash my mother's body.

We're going to wash our mother's dead body.
This we could have answered,
the unadorned fact.

2.

In my hand I hold a white cloth;
in my hand I lift my mother's arm,
draw the cloth from her armpit—
the dusky hairs—along the tender flesh
like a sea creature beached—past elbow
to her wrist, the magnificent hinge of her body.
What beautiful skin she has my sister says.

Yes. I draw the cloth over the lines and mounts,
eternal, they say, corrupt. I take each finger,
the arthritic knuckles, abalone nails, into my hand—

I need this holding, this bearing of weightlessness.
We pass our cloths over her breasts and under.
They've grown too little to lap our hands. And so
to belly, groin, thighs. We spray
blossoms on her neck, on her breasts,
on her wrists, fine-boned and sure, on the soles
of her feet. So it is done.

ON ONE RIVER WE LISTEN TO
MUSIC OF ANOTHER RIVER

We take turns tossing your ashes with a painted cup—
purple violets, a spring flower, hardy, despite
seeming frail—though I reach in to touch your ash.

Our bodies are cool in the May breeze, swallows
sweep insects before them, cars trundle across
the bridge upriver from where we stand on sand.

After we let your ashes go, a few of us stay
to listen to The Moldau on a boombox, the sound
loosed in the outdoors. Years before, you and our father

left us with a babysitter and drove to the river,
to be alone, to fish and drink, to argue, probably,
and take turns reading to one another.

You turned on the engine of the car
so that you could listen to music, public radio,
and the two of you undressed and lay down

in the music and touched one another and wept,
because you wept at music no matter how tender
or how bold, and The Moldau was both, hunters

chasing a fox and nymphs bathing by moonlight
in the river's flowing waters, pale and steady,
the music swirling and unspooling,

so we listened to Smetana as your ashes flowed
and our father, who is with us, is
with you, in that summer when mosquitoes

weren't too bad, and the river rippled and spun
in the moonlight, and touching you was sweet
and slow and muddy and enough.

GIFT

We say we are giving you to the river
and then we correct ourselves and say

it is your ashes we give. We say give
because toss is too casual, because throw

suggests a target. There is a breeze.
Some of the ashes do not go directly

into the water. Some blow back onto
our knees. This is not your body, this fine

gray stuff that mingles with the fine
fluff of cottonwood seeds. So we say

we give your ash to the river, though
what or who is doing the possessing—where

are you to have ash, as if the ash belongs
to you, and you are not the ash. And who

are we to give this ash which is both
yours and not yours, you and not you,

to the river. And what is the river to receive
you with open hands—

yes, the river stands before us
with open hands, not at all certain

what gift this is, but willing to receive it,
and it does reach out to take the ash,

to take it from us, like an old woman
who takes your wounded body and binds

it up with eddy and current and watery shroud
and so we turn our backs and are healed.

4: Detour

NINE DETOURS ON THE RIVER

Around any body,
across burnished water,
swallows soar.

*

Coursing over sandbar
current casts
such recklessness.

*

The river folds itself,
makes flowers of leaves,
returns to water.

*

Rain overnight—the tree's submerged,
the river moves,
is its own detour.

*

To plumb current
waves fold the shadow's paths.
Here or there just the same.

*

I know the heron by shadow.
Roots of a cottonwood above water:
no shadow.

*

Turtle surfaces, tries the bank
and doesn't move.
Teach me to surface.

*

Along the bank, sunlight.
Days of no rain.
Have I changed so soon?

*

How vain to seek certainty.
Teach me,
cloud, ash, heron's shadow.

MAKING AND NOT MAKING

On the day a loved one dies
anything is possible. All

that is is something else.
The voices of the living

resemble the voices of the dead.
Nothing is familiar

when you turn back
to where you were.

You look down and
your hands are your mother's.

Laughing and crying
are indistinguishable.

All the doors open and
whether you walk through or not,

your path is the same.

SOME MORNINGS

I wake and know
you've been with me

in the night
while bats move through air

collecting mosquitoes, and stars
fall and never land.

Your voice—
how can I not

hear it in daylight hours.
If it knocks against

the membrane of day
I am deaf to it.

NOCTURNE

Alone on the glacial lake—a bowl
abandoned 10,000 years ago
and deep enough to stay a record of itself—
the world is mine.
No birds, no leaping fish, day's door ajar.

I'd tell you this if you were here.

A fawn newly-hatched and spindled
follows a doe, the two placid as moons.
They step in shallow water silent
as meteors until they come to reeds—
a cloistered world—and thus I am alone again.

HAVING CHOSEN THE NEAR BANK

Water flows wide and thin
between ice, the deeper ice
yellow and coursed by silt,

ice above blue, luminous, like sky
on the river. Today it's overcast,
no shadows, no reflections.

My breath makes clouds.

It's too cold to stand on the bridge.
I flow between seasons, sieve
what I've ported past barn and sheafs

of cattails, past beaver lodge and powerline.
I feel the inevitable
rising up, wide, thin.

I GAVE MY GRIEF

I gave my grief
to the heron,

the penstemon,
the rivers' current,

the shadow
of what I missed seeing—

bird already flown—

the seed
caught by wind,

dropped beyond my path,

to what stays the same—
and here I pause,

for always
there is no permanence—

I gave my grief
to what flows past

writhing, wrinkling,
folding into itself, wrestling the earth.

UNRESOLVED DETOUR

I was in a hurry—
presto!—across the prairie—
seeking her voice—
how she called from the kitchen
tempo! that's too fast—
how she cussed and horse-laughed—
to ease the tension—
how she sang
before emphysema.

I was in a hurry
but it was detour season—
hot days of tar and startled pitch,
girls in ratcheted yellow,
men in steel-toed boots
using their work-ironed hands
to tell us where to go.

A detour took me out of time
onto a path I can not retrace.

I was in a hurry—
the river could not come too soon.

TOUR

There the room where our friend
cried all day and broke

a lead-weighted window
with his bare hand. Here

the grief we carry in our fists.
There praise, here despair.

There a garter snake slipped across
my path and into wild rhubarb.

Here I wander empty rooms
opening my hands. Empty

I go to the alley to stand
below the full moon. I knock

and knock and grow afraid.
A dog barks down the block

and my ears are opened—
bees in the neighbor's lilac.

BLUES FOR DISASTER

In the park, someone plays a Hammond
under a white canopy, thirds and fourths
in no hurry to return home. The blues
don't take you home 'til you're good and ready.

Years before, in '98, a tornado clawhammered
the elm we'd once climbed on a dare. I was long gone
in '98. My parents had gone then, my siblings too,
to other states. We missed the disaster.

The guy next door cranks on his lawnmower.
I think of the maple's blazing shade, its girth,
the brown bat we chased out the kitchen door,
how it clung to the maple all afternoon, black eyes open.

These blues aren't my blues but I sing along,
watch the neighbor pace up and down, tighten
the arc nearer, nearer his trees. From this
distance all disasters are beautiful.

RESTLESS NOCTURNE

Every memory of you is fixed—notes
on a stave, moving and permanent,
held together only by listening,
as in a private entranced playing of Chopin.
Other times the music's fitful, broken.
White cowbane tips toward swallows.
Between weeping petals a slender beetle
makes its way. I can sit on this bank
where we let you go, fixed by light
slanting and hungry, by swallows
dropping their breasts acrobatic and quick
onto the river's surface, by the blackbird
picking among reeds. I can wait like this
through the day, into dusk, I can stay all night.

LOOKING AT THIS PHOTOGRAPH

I can smell your forehead
at the hairline—how soft
your hair, tickling—
like a mouse's nest. Your jaw

is set, something serious being said
outside the photo, away from us,
you here in this photograph,
me holding it, trying

to shorten the distance. Once,
when you lay against a hospital bed,
I massaged lotion across
your shoulders—knobs of bone there

like rhubarb nosing up into spring—
and across your sternum,
between your breasts, your soft body
nurturing even as it was dying.

I DREAM OF MY DEAD MOTHER (1)

All morning you've been sitting on a stool
in the pantry, the iron bean pot on the floor nearby,
jars of pickles like the ghosts of Baptists come
to wag: For shame. For shame.

Beyond the room that should be the kitchen
is an auditorium, empty, except
for all the people on the stage in paisley silk
and tattered linen with drinks in one hand

and skewered meat or cigarettes in the other
and the men use their height and the women
their hips or cleavage to clear
a space in what's given. Three bats circle

and circle, heedless of all that fucking genius
on the stage. In the pantry, on the difficult stool
under the one raw bulb, you begin to sing.
You sing Puccini, the melody he couldn't slough;

it could score your veins with its blade of longing.
Come out, I call to you in the dream, my voice
full of iron and salt, come out,
the moon has risen, they've gone away.

ANY WAY A DETOUR

Isoprene lines on the river
curled, jinked,
swallows fell from the bridges' eaves,
fell against the mapped
surface. Here

your bodily remains
began their passage,
turning and thinning against
the river's vellum, succumbing
to the current.

And no map
remains. No way
to follow. Or let us say
there is nothing
but detours.

HERON ASYLUM IN THE CROWNS OF COTTONWOODS

Through binoculars I watched
a heron rookery inland
from the ash-bank, nests sky-facing,
a dozen, and chicks in each, their eyes
black planets. It *is a curious
and rather anomalous circumstance
that the herons, which are decidedly
waders, and formed for walking,
should build and roost on trees,
where their motions are all awkward.*

It was said herons were fat
at the full moon and lean at the new,
as women fatten to readiness
and then lie fallow. It was said
a heron would eat an eel which
would swim through, and the heron
would eat it again, an infinite passage,
an ouroboros through dark to light and back.

The herons above made few sounds,
a cough, nothing like the *hollow
screams* of other seasons. And each
by one raised her great wings and
pushed down as if to birth herself
direct into the sky. And then she'd
leave, her *long legs stretched out in a right
line behind her like a tail and probably
serving the same rudder-like office.*
The chicks stared out over the scrambled
nests, already practicing patience, since

the heron practices *the most unwearied*
patience in fishing. Her *stroke is quick*
as thought and sure as fate.

My back against a tree,
I wasn't watching this fishing,
only the patient coming and going,
the standing high up in cottonwoods surrounded
by a greeny slough far back from the current
we'd given my mother's ashes to, far back from
the fresh grief. I was not practicing patience,
my practice was love. I moved among the birds
above, parents tall, aloof, "exhibiting
the picture of wretchedness" as Buffon wrote,
though what did he know. The chicks
had the knob heads of old men, the adults
the crook eye of children. I joined them
in a convivial boundered world,
and when I pulled the binoculars away
I was lost.

INSIDE A GIFT

Inside a gift
is something
unexpected

just as
inside a shell
is the sound
of the unseen

inside
my heart
is your voice

inside a snowflake
an entire storm

inside an oxbow
the river's direction

inside morning
is evening.

5: From the shadow

SHADOW OF THE RIVER'S COURSE

Such restlessness

around any body—

heron's shadow, cloud, ash—

a swallow soars across

burnished water—plumbs current—

waves fold the shadow's path.

A PURPLE RAVELLING

Anyhow, with no warning, the radio
powdered away to a low buzz, a pewter
undertow of sound, then with one loud
rasp across the sky, a shimmer of light
pure as anodyne, the car went silent
lost in a high-pressure zone, then a low,
enough to turn the sky inside out,
ravel it before my very eyes. I drove on
along the section line, corn in rows
vary-less as if someone had crossed the road
enervated and mathematical and had
lost themselves in this parallel universe.
Lost myself, anyhow, in watching across
instant repetition, row, row, row, rain
nervously slanting across the windshield
going nowhere, going right on down the road.

HOW WE CAN SURVIVE TO WINTER

Sky sips the blue mist
that collars shriveled leadplant
and raveled web.

The mist doesn't last,
succumbs to sun's
first commands.

Purple liatris throw
open their shutters
to tarrying hummingbirds.

Mink and muskrat
cross the river's rug
from bank to bank.

A high thermal embraces
hawk as if they'd been
desperate for one another.

Winter sent its one word telegram.
To mark the way
big bluestem darkens.

The hawk abandons
the high sky,
a slight turn, a feint.

I DREAM OF MY DEAD MOTHER (2)

We were smoking beside the house,
between windows,
a big house on a hill, an unfamiliar house,
rooftops below and low clouds miles away.
I could have fallen
into what was not seen.

I was naked, my arms
crossed over my breasts,
the house the color of our skin,
we smoked and shivered and she was naked, too,
her belly drooping like bunting,
her pubic hair thinned to pale weeds,
we smoked together, away from the windows,
so that we would not be seen.

NOCTURNE FOR THE BODY

We scavenged for wild grapes
and driftwood, the time-worn, water-
worn grain beyond change,
and in our wandering we'd come on shacks
men from the state hospital
had quilted out of what they found
washed up or tossed out, hermit-houses
they'd made in the cottonwood
and viney universe, away from correctives
and strait-jackets, away from the violent ones
who stored piss below their iron beds
and called to a god who answered from the radiators.

These men we never saw.
They were off collecting water for geraniums in coffee cans,
digging out a yard of rusted ornamental fence
beached from upriver. They were sleeping
on a sand bank, under the brazen sun.
We'd look through plastic-sheathed windows
to study their lives, how neat the margins.
On All-Saints' Day they moved up
off the flood plain, back into the wards.
The simple poured concrete of their graves
was stamped only with the numbers
they'd been assigned when they were delivered.

WHAT THE DEAD DO FOR THE LIVING

I.

At the bottom of the chest freezer—
below catfish filets in tin foil, elk sausage
and deer tongue, below a stash of twenties
in a juice can, below a blue coffee tin
of walnut cookies, a half gallon bucket
labeled in red ink on masking tape "for pie or jam, '86,"
found by my aunt's daughters weeks after her death,
lifted out, resurrected, the last thing, all else
moved to other freezers or the garbage, this preserved fruit
"still bright and fresh" one cousin wrote to all of us,
fruit picked twenty-six years before
from seedling trees my aunt and uncle planted
fifty years ago—thawed and cooked,
"as well as we remember how she did it,"
my cousin wrote—were apricots for cobbler.

2.

Cobbler in a jelly roll pan, enough to feed
Coxey's Army, a lost memory,
enough to feed the old people in the nursing home,
one of them my cousins' father, to whom
they carried the cobbler, the pan labeled beneath
in black ink on masking tape, "Owen," the cobbler
something bright and fresh, and on the way,
driving across western Missouri grassland,
my cousin, the one who remembered and told,
counted a red-tailed hawk, a flock

of snow geese, two coots circling in a stock pond,
all the bird life daring in its simplicity,
the aroma of apricots and cinnamon
filling the car in the way the dead
can suddenly arrive and fill the room.

3.

A decade before my uncle recuperated
in the Missouri nursing home, he climbed,
with some of his brothers and their wives,
to where they could see the Mississippi
flow—a bright dare—across the driftless,
and the effigy mounds, some shaped like birds—
a heron, a hawk, a goose—others like bear or turtle,
to where they saw prairie spread westward
in long waves, and there he spoke—fervent
as an animal—of having been in that place before,
as if he knew those who'd shaped the earth
and buried their people, as if they were around
him, around them, above hawk and heron,
in this place where glaciers never came to scour
the earth, as if he were home, surrounded by the dead.

4.

A year later he was gone, sung over,
swung over, lifted out of his bed
and carried off, and we were hushed.
It was January, in Missouri. Snow
banked the fields. Those who could
had gone south—hawks and herons
and coots—and we gathered,

most of the old people in our clan gone
or unable, we gathered, the next generation
and our children, to make space for
one another. We walked the road
where the apricot trees stood naked,
a clear night sky enough of an effigy
for the time, and among us, sure it is,
sure, the dead arrived, bright and fresh.

SHADOW THAT SETTLES AGAINST ITS SUBSTANCE

Not the light, but light's memory.

Not the grave, but the stone.

Not the mouth, the ear, the wound.

Not what I carry, but what is lifted from me.

The intimacies of sandbank,
of ash on wind, of leaf and seed
borne downstream.

Not my mother's voice.

The mouth opens to sorrow,
the ear to shadow's course,
the wound to willow.

ELEMENTAL (5)

There is a kind of beauty ample
in its gift—

sunlight after weeks
of winter overcast—

singer's pull out of
and into the heart's cavity—

earth from space
and from earth a glimpse of space—

and, too, a beauty simple,
announced by nothing but itself—

the first dandelion,
the last candle snuffed—

clouds on water,
the cleanliness of grief.

WHAT WAKENS IN US

This morning wind trips
over itself to get where it's going.

Clematis lean east slightly moist,
mums blush sky's pink.

You hesitate. Your presence
might shatter something.

Four crows on a telephone line
squawk twice and fall into air.

6: Weight of a body

COURSES (ON THE RIVER)COURSE

I knew the heron by shadow.

            a cottonwood
water,   above water.

shadows' paths.

to plumb your current,

      ash—

        Turtle surfaces, tries the bank

      water.

current—   sandbar.

Rain over the tree's   submerged—

     detour.

The river folds itself.
        bank.   sunlight.

                                   no rain.

           the bank, body—

makes flow   water—

How vain to seek   just   the   same.

Rain overnight—the tree's submerged.

the river   vain to seek certainty.

is in own   Teach me.   To   plumb   current

          cloud, ash, heron's   the shadow's   paths.

        Here or there

                    just the same.

QUESTIONS FOR THE ELEMENTAL COURSE

What is the sound of a bird falling?

Do we hear wings more clearly at night?

Aquinas said our souls have weight.
    What is the weight of the night's soul?
    Of the soul of the heron?

What is the smell of night? the recklessness of current?

My sister sends a copy of a recipe for mustard in our mother's hand.
    On the back she had written—our mother—Wake me up
    when you get up. Please.

Can we feel the night pass, as we might a cloth thrown across
    a table?
How many bells answer the night's demands?

Where does a fold begin?

How many times must we surface to know we have arrived?

What is the weight of mourning? the length of the heron's course?

Saturn has 62 moons, 9 without names.
    How do we name the night? the soul?

Is the night a wrinkle, a ringing, a ripeness?

Do we dare tempt the margins?

The glacier booms and echoes, spills its thousand flints,
its frilled dust.
How many years has it plunged uncanny and beautiful?

The trunk brought down from the attic smells of raisins
and blue ink, of the bodies our ancestors lived in.
What is the weight of an abandoned body?

Can we know the night by heart?

If I hold you all night, —— ?

The moon wrinkles in water, splits open like ripe fruit.
What is the weight of a body dropped into water?

NOTES

"Nocturne for January, 1965"
  The italicized lines are from a Vietnam protest song sung by
  Country Joe & the Fish.

"A Purple Ravelling"
  This poem is an acrostic built on a phrase from poem #219 of
  Emily Dickinson

"Shadow that Settles Against Its Substance"
  "Secure the shadow ere the substance fade, let nature imitate
  what nature made" was an advertising slogan used by early
  photographers.

"The Patience of Job"
  Lines come from The Book of Job in the King James edition
  of the *Bible*.

"Heron Asylum in the Crowns of Cottonwoods"
  Italicized lines are from *American Ornithology: or, The Natural
  History of North America,* Alexander Wilson and Prince
  Charles Lucien Bonaparte. Pronouns have been changed.
  Buffon was a French naturalist of the 18th Century. He
  defined genius as "a greater aptitude for patience."

ACKNOWLEDGMENTS

Poems in this manuscript first appeared (sometimes in slightly different form) in:

Cider Press Review: "Asylum," "On One River We Listen to Music of Another River"
Drunken Boat: "What Can Be Made of Nothing"
Flyway: "I Gave My Grief," "I Had to Wait," "Departure (was "Turtle")
ISLE: "Elemental (1)" (was "Driving")
Literary Bohemian: "Blues Nocturne"
Mezzo Cammin: "Nocturne," "Song"
One (Jacar): "Three Scenes in Search of History"
Talking Writing: "Having Chosen the Near Bank"
Tar River Poetry:"Mornings Before the Texas High-Noon Heat" (was "Laundry")
Tinderbox Poetry Journal: "How We Can Survive to Winter"
Umbrella: "The Sharp Distance (2)" (was "Oxygen")
Up the Staircase Quarterly: "Making and Not Making," "Shadow that Settles Against Itself"
Valparaiso Poetry Review: "Asters," "Elemental (2)" (was "Nocturne"), "Tenderness," "Evening Rite"
Water-Stone Review: "On the River After the Sun Goes Down"
Zone 3: "Cursing the Cold"

"Nothing Stays the Same on the River" was included in the anthology *Down to the Dark River* (Louisiana Literature Press, Philip C. Kolin and Jack B. Bedell, editors)

Six of the poems in this book were set as a song cycle entitled "I Give Voice to My Mother" by the Minnesota composer Linda Kachelmeier. Thank you, Linda, for seeing to the core of this book with such power and beauty.

Most of all I want to thank Margaret Hasse, Lise Kildegaard, James Moore, Su Smallen, Jessica Piazza, and Elizabeth Tannen for what you've taught me about this book; the muses of WompWorks for insight into particular poems; Molly Sutton Kiefer for leading *Course* into the world; Nikkita Cohoon for making it beautiful; and Arne, because our courses intertwine and I'm glad of that.

I wish to acknowledge that an Artist Initiative Grant from the Minnesota State Arts Board in 2010 was fundamental to the writing of this book.

Athena Kildegaard's previous books are *Rare Momentum*, *Bodies of Light* (a finalist for the Minnesota Book Award), *Cloves & Honey* (a finalist for the Midwest Book Award), and *Ventriloquy*. She received the LRAC/McKnight Fellowship and grants from the Lake Region Arts Council and the Minnesota State Arts Board. She teaches at the University of Minnesota, Morris.